PENGUIN BOOKS

THE PURITY OF DESIRE

JALALUDDIN RUMI (1207–1273) is one of the greatest poets known to history. For nearly eight hundred years he has had an astounding influence throughout the Islamic world, and more recently in Western countries. Born in Vakhsh (in present day Tajikistan), in what was then considered the eastern edge of the Persian empire, Rumi is currently one of the most widely read poets in the English language. The son of a scholar, jurist, and mystic, Rumi succeeded his father as the sheik of a divinity college. At the age of thirty-seven his sober life as a teacher was irrevocably changed upon meeting the wandering mystic of astonishing presence, Shams-e Tabriz, whom Rumi recognized as a doorway to God. Shams became Rumi's beloved companion and Master, and thus began an indefinable relationship of divine longing and union. Rumi's tremendous creative outpouring of verse was born from his love for Shams. In fully identifying with and honoring his Master, Rumi called his largest work, a 40,000-verse collection of lyric poetry, the *Divan-e Shams-e Tabriz*. Love is the essence of Rumi, love became his very being, the impetus of all his poetry. Rumi sings fantastic promises that do not disappoint the sincere student. "Stand with dignity in the magnificent current of my words and they will carry you into God's arms."

DANIEL LADINSKY is one of the most successful living writers in the world working with poetry. His work has reached millions of people. Daniel lived in India for six years, where he worked in a rural clinic free to the poor, and was a student of the essence and unity of all faiths. Ladinsky's other books include *A Year with Hafiz: Daily Contemplations, The Gift, Love Poems from God, The Subject Tonight Is Love*, and *I Heard God Laughing*. Once, when Daniel was asked a reason for his accomplishments and if he had any advice for other artists, he quoted a line from an old Broadway musical that went "You gotta have heart, miles and miles and miles of heart!"

The Purity
of
Desire

100 POEMS OF
Rumi

DANIEL LADINSKY
WITH NANCY OWEN BARTON

PENGUIN BOOKS

PENGUIN BOOKS
Published by the Penguin Group
Penguin Group (USA) Inc., 375 Hudson Street, New York, New York 10014, USA
Penguin Group (Canada), 90 Eglinton Avenue East, Suite 700, Toronto, Ontario M4P 2Y3, Canada
(a division of Pearson Penguin Canada Inc.)
Penguin Books Ltd, 80 Strand, London WC2R 0RL, England
Penguin Ireland, 25 St Stephen's Green, Dublin 2, Ireland (a division of Penguin Books Ltd)
Penguin Group (Australia), 707 Collins Street, Melbourne, Victoria 3008, Australia
(a division of Pearson Australia Group Pty Ltd)
Penguin Books India Pvt Ltd, 11 Community Centre, Panchsheel Park,
New Delhi – 110 017, India
Penguin Group (NZ), 67 Apollo Drive, Rosedale, Auckland 0632, New Zealand
(a division of Pearson New Zealand Ltd)
Penguin Books, Rosebank Office Park, 181 Jan Smuts Avenue,
Parktown North 2193, South Africa
Penguin China, B7 Jaiming Center, 27 East Third Ring Road North,
Chaoyang District, Beijing 100020, China

Penguin Books Ltd, Registered Offices:
80 Strand, London WC2R 0RL, England

First published in Penguin Books 2012

5   7   9   10   8   6   4

"The Body is Like Mary" appeared in the journal, *Lalitamba*.
"Isn't That Something?" appeared in Daniel Ladinsky's *Love Poems
from God* (Penguin Books, 2002).
The afterword, "A Note on Divinity" appeared in Mr. Ladinsky's *The Subject
Tonight is Love* (Pumpkin House, 1996).

LIBRARY OF CONGRESS CATALOGING-IN-PUBLICATION DATA
Jalal al-Din Rumi, Maulana, 1207–1273.
[Selections. English. 2012]
The purity of desire : 100 poems of Rumi / [edited and translated by]
Daniel Ladinsky : with Nancy Owen Barton.
p.   cm.
Translated from Persian.
ISBN 978-0-14-312161-9
I. Ladinsky, Daniel James.   II. Barton, Nancy Owen.   III. Title.
PK6480. E5L33 2012
891'.5511—dc23
2012035950

Printed in the United States of America

ALWAYS LEARNING   PEARSON

The body is like Mary, and
each of us has a Jesus inside.

—RUMI

To my eyes, lovers touching are
folded wings in a beautiful prayer.

—RUMI

ACKNOWLEDGMENTS

As my eighty-five-year-old, sweet mom recently said to me, "You know Danny, it still amazes me to see your name on books." And I replied, "It amazes me too, mom." With that in mind, having an acknowledgment page to write can at first be confusing. But here goes: Foremost, great thanks to those mentioned in the Introduction, which of course includes my agent and friend, Nancy Barton.

Thanks to Jeff Wolverton, *an old lover of God*, who has been a wonderful gardener and caretaker, for about 40 years, at the spiritual center I often visit. Jeff brought a couple of my favorite lines in this book to my attention that I then worked with, expounded upon. He has danced with Rumi a long time; I think Rumi would call Jeff . . . *kin*.

Elizabeth Heaney's help was very timely, skilled and appreciated. She knows something about real love, and giving it.

Kara Gilligan, Gervaise Christiansen and Joan Body generously gave their finely honed talents to the design and layout of this book. Hugs to each of you.

It may be an odd thing to thank, but I think I should . . . a broken heart I have had for several years now from losing the two warm-blooded creatures I was closest to. It is some rare balance between the extremes, I think a work like this requires: on one side, a heart so tender it can weep in a moment from sadness and all the suffering in the world, and on the other side—there's wild humor and *an eye* that can seemingly (with just a tiny flex of inner will) behold great splendor. That is where I camp these days, between those poles. I plow a field there. Songs rise. They filled this book, the best I could.

Carolyn Carlson, my editor at Penguin, has stuck by me for seven years now. She has been remarkable, always encouraging. Thanks, thanks, thanks to you, C.

And for maybe the next one hundred years, I think any significant book in English, with Rumi's name on it, should honor Coleman Barks. I am glad for the opportunity. He has done some fantastic trailblazing and may even get nominated for the Nobel Prize in Literature. I will close this with a few words from one of Coleman's Rumi poems that I just put into my own blender, and tinkered with—as I do:

Our whole life seeks one kiss, God's mouth to ours.
Hard to imagine a more befitting welcome to eternity.

CONTENTS

THE WING COMES ALIVE IN HIS PRESENCE

I was recently asked if I could explain the Rumi phenomenon in the Western world in just one line. I thought for a few moments, then replied, *"Well, maybe, but could I quote Hafiz?"* And the person smiled, knowing of my work with that other great Persian poet. The line was

> *The wing comes alive in his presence.*

I think that is it, something of the answer. The wing, *the soul,* the heart, comes alive in the presence of a real teacher. And we all live to feel alive, don't we? It seems to me our every moment is about that—wanting, needing, to experience *life* as fully as we can.

> *Loving is the greatest freedom and fulfillment, so the wise, being wise, cash in on that.*

We are all addicted to happiness, and that can serve us well, if we then go about achieving it in what might be called spiritual or humanistic, organic ways. Which basically means: we utilize our intelligence in making decisions that affect our bodies, our minds, and others. Therein, the tremendous value of Rumi. He helps each of us to become more of a friend—first to one's self and to those close. Then, if one has the capacity, one might begin to enrich one's local community, country of residence, and perhaps even touch the world with their talents.

There is not a minute in the day when we are not trying, really the best we can, to have a sense of well-being with all the trimmings. Whatever circumstance we find ourselves in, we do try to make the best of it. But that does not mean we might, at times, maybe even often, turn things into a mess. Here again, the value of a teacher, or just a smart friend: they help us to keep the mop in the closet more. Then we can spend less time repairing our hearts and aspects of our lives, because we are becoming less entangled with that which may impede. Yes, well-being with all its trimmings—of peace, fun, laughter, and a deeper, more intense engagement in work, play, passions, contentment—all that starts to become the norm in our days.

> *The true gauge of success and functioning intellect is having what you want. Otherwise, are you not at war with conflicts and the unrequited?*

Rumi is perfect for a country like America, with its national symbol of an eagle, and its Wild West heritage and *sacks full of assertions and desires*. He is a wonderful diplomat from the Mountain, from the Sun, for any nation or individual who cherishes ideals, liberty, vitality, and zest. And for the artist, Rumi may be that rare instructor and guide, having himself made one of the greatest creative outpourings in recorded history with his verse.

All external action of the human being is traceable back to some internal, spiritual need. Each of us goes out into the world and bucks heads with it, in some way—providing what shelter and nourishment we can for our families, for the precious we hold, once felt, or deeply believe in. We are all trying to create that space, the environment, where truth, or the height of our experience, can happen again or anew. We want to fully relax and breathe in as much beauty as we can. We want to feel, think ... *Hey, that was joy that just stopped in for a visit! Glad it came by. I was wondering where the hell it had been.*

The taste of God, the wonderful scent of the Nameless, we somehow know. And being governed, in a way, by such a scent, we become blessed and ruined by its memory. But how can we not crave that?

I think we are using all our wits to enter some inner sky again where we once played with the Divine. But our senses, our abilities to know more of our Self, are broken in places—caged, cracked, sheared, and often denied. That is why we cry. That is why there are wars. That is why there is hatred, why we fear and know greed. That is why a life can seem so empty and hopeless at times, and this surely must add to and perpetuate anyone's desperation, or depression.

Good poetry, like music or a sweet touch, can doctor us up, be an antidote for an hour or longer, help us to get dressed for another day—combat the blues enough to mount the horse again; and maybe even aid one in laying down the insidious weight of some old grudge or deep-rooted anxiety. Herein enters Rumi.

O yeah, here comes Rumi, with a chuck wagon full of all kinds of stuff. Everything the guy serves is perfectly cooked and draws us near to his—*and our own*—inner light. His startling synergy of images germinates Realization. From head to toe this guy is blazing. He is like a cyclone one wants to be drawn into, though at the same time, one can feel rightfully hesitant. Yet, the treasuries in this world are spotted close when in his presence. And then someone yells, "*Gold! There is fucking gold everywhere!*" Which about covers things for a while. No complaints are heard. Crowd control in the immediate area is achieved. Rumi can do that, help any—even the whole world—to lay down the *guns*, that we all carry, one way or another.

But Rumi is not satisfied with little miracles. So the party gets cranked up more as he keeps dancing, and all of a sudden the wagon master shouts,

> *When I am done with you, the firmament will be smeared all over your face; even your asshole will be a shrine.*

And some, hearing such ribald language, sing back,

> *Thank God! Thank God! Hallelujah, baby, someone just told me the truth.*

But then a few others walk away, thinking,

Blasphemy, how could every part of me be holy?

What to say? It has been long known: good poetry is also meant for the high rollers in the barroom where the talk gets gritty and real— as well as for the pious in the mosque, temple, and church.

Jalaluddin Rumi (1207–1273) and My History with Him

I feel the English-speaking countries are very fortunate to now have the name and verse of Rumi spoken in many of their homes and gathering places. For any who might want more knowledge of Jalaluddin Rumi and the many available translations of his poems, there is a wealth of credible information available in print and on the Internet. There has been exceptional research and writing about Rumi's life and poetry for over a century now in English. You will find some of those sources listed in the bibliography at the end of this book.

I have worked with Rumi before. I published some twenty-five renderings of his verse in a best-selling anthology from Penguin called *Love Poems from God*. A few of those earliest published Rumi poems have gotten a lot of attention. One very short poem was transformed into a ten-page choral piece that was sung on tour throughout Europe by an internationally known young women's choir. Here is that poem that just seems so true. Truth, and a freshness, and charm, being the needed hallmarks, to my mind, of any successful translation or rendering:

I like when the music happens like this: Something in His eye grabs holds of a tambourine in me,

then I turn and lift a violin in someone else, and they turn, and this turning continues, it has reached you now – isn't that something?

I first came across the name Rumi, forty years ago, back in my college days in Arizona, while reading a book called *God Speaks*, by Meher Baba. I was struck by Rumi then and have reprinted the first poem of his I ever saw, as the opening poem in this book. It was about twenty years later before Rumi again came into my life in any significant way. So, I will tell this story for any who may be interested, for Rumi seems to be a real connection, a bridge if you will, to my work with Hafiz, which has dominated my life for many years now.

It was in October 1992 that my second real encounter with Rumi happened. I was in India, on one of my many visits there, and I was seated near a man I considered to be my (living) spiritual teacher. I guess most people want to think they have a great teacher. But this man, whom we simply called Eruch, was indeed exceptional and had capabilities that I felt were really impossible for any ordinary human being.* An example: I feel the most sophisticated and staunch atheist could have sat before him, and if Eruch wanted—with a blink of his eye—he could have that person weeping in gratitude for the experience of *divine tenderness* caressing them, or for actually seeing something they would then call *God*. The real teacher, I feel, has access to all possibilities *riding* in his or her pockets, that can be easily pulled out, utilized.

This man, Eruch, was also co-author of that book, *God Speaks*, under the direct supervision of Meher Baba. Baba, who had stopped writing at this juncture, and had not spoken for many years, would meticulously dictate points to Eruch, using an alphabet board or a unique sign language. Eruch would then write down those points, expanding upon them where he felt Baba wanted him to. Later, he

---

* Eruch Byramshaw Jessawala was born in India, October 13, 1916, and became one of Meher Baba's closest disciples. Eruch first met Meher Baba when he was nine years old and later joined his "circle of intimate companions" at the age of 21. Eternal Beloved, a beautiful 40-minute DVD (available from Sheriar Books), shows some wonderful scenes of Eruch's life with Meher Baba. Eruch passed away on August 31, 2001, at a place called Meherazad, in western India, a desert oasis where he had lived for many years with Baba, and where Eruch then personally greeted and interacted with thousands of people from around the world, often affecting them deeply, after Baba's passing, in 1969.

and Baba would go over everything Eruch had written, in the greatest of detail.

I want to say, too, that although I think Eruch could be extraordinarily intriguing on his own, he almost always preferred to *teach* via stories of his profoundly intimate life with Meher Baba. On some occasions, though, he would instruct by telling the stories of historic great saints or by having their poetry read aloud.

So here I am, seated around this beautiful man (probably a true saint himself), and he is wearing, as he usually did, a simple T-shirt with his perpetual funky, baggy pants. Some very no-bullshit, hip people are eyeing him like delighted bees who just found a pristine meadow in bloom. And Eruch says to a Westerner who is close to him, Gary Kleiner, who is a beloved spiritual son, "Gary, would you read to me today?"

Gary responds, "Sure, what would you like to hear?"

"Would you mind reading to us some Rumi?" asks Eruch.

Now, I had spent time with Eruch, off and on, for nearly fifteen years at this point. At the time of this incident, I was a guest of his, at a very private household where he lived. I had never known Eruch to call for Rumi when I was around him. But here I am, on this day I am describing, and here too is Gary, who has a very fine theatrical reading voice and is now holding this particular Rumi book. He starts to look through it to find a poem to read, but Eruch reaches over and gently takes the book out of his hand, saying, "I will show you what I would like to hear today." And my little Western brain starts thinking … *this should be interesting.*

So, Gary starts to read and gets through maybe half of a poem. I can't remember which one it was, for my mind did a kind of somersault and lost its normal ability to function. What I do remember, as if I were there right now, is the effect the poem had on me: I was stunned by its beauty. I felt like I was face to face with God in words, as much as God can be in words. I realized in a second that this was the first time in my life I was hearing poetry and the first time in my life I felt a deep connection with it. I was overwhelmed. Then another poem was read, and what

I was listening to was literally snapping my head back in amazement, as if something invisible was kicking me with sacred hoofs. Then, a third Rumi poem was read, and now I was just sitting there, zapped to my core, wonderfully dazed. Eruch then reached over, took the book from Gary and (in his ever perfect poise) said thanks to him. Some tea he had ordered for us arrived, and the mood became very light as Eruch steered the conversation away from what was just read.

What happened the day following my first *hearing* of poetry, I have told before in some detail, in an essay I wrote called *Releasing the Spirit of Hafiz*, published in two of my Hafiz books: *I Heard God Laughing* and *A Year with Hafiz*. And although it may have seemed natural to have first started working with Rumi, the very next day I got plugged deep into Hafiz, from a conversation with Eruch that changed my life.

A TEAR FALLS ON ME

Dreams have been important to me at times, and I still value a few very much. I have had perhaps twenty in my life, thus far, that I feel were truly significant, even milestones. I did have one dream which involved Rumi that was touching, and I think of importance. Shortly after this dream, I began to render some of his work in preparation for the book I mentioned, *Love Poems from God*. That dream went like this:

I was seated in a beautiful auditorium that had its main floor sloping toward the stage, and there was balcony seating also. In this auditorium, which could have held a few hundred people, there were only a dozen or so scattered about, watching (my guess is) a marvelous play. At least most there seemed to be watching the play. All of my attention, though, was really focused on Eruch, who was seated almost alone, some two or three rows in front of me and off to the left a bit. So I am really just looking at him— but he is watching the play, and the play is about Rumi. And while some lines of Rumi are being read by the actor playing him, Eruch starts to weep because of the exquisiteness of the poetry. I can see tears rolling down the right side of his cheek, and I have never seen Eruch cry before. Then all of a sudden, my face becomes close to Eruch's, it is beneath his, and a tear of his love for Rumi falls on me.

My work with Rumi in this book is much like my work with Hafiz. Primarily, I try to make the spirit of this great poet as alive, contemporary, giving, and tangible, as possible. Many of these poems here were greatly aided by an old friend and my current agent, Nancy Owen Barton. Nancy has long been connected with my work, bears a lasting love of the poetry and lives of Rumi and Hafiz, and has been a student of Sufism. In the early stages of this book, she would often send me Rumi verse from literal translations in the public domain that she felt I might enhance and expound upon, as no others working with Rumi had, up to this point. Nancy also made some wonderful poetic contributions to a few of these poems. On occasion, I simply reworked Rumi poems she had crafted. At times, she tried keeping me closer to the scholarly bone, but still I often veered when I felt it would best serve the verse artistically or help reveal certain aspects to contemporary readers. A line attributed to Hafiz comes to mind in regards to this:

No one could ever paint a too wonderful
picture of my heart or God.

I feel this is very true of Rumi. And that is my goal—to try to reveal, as much as possible, Rumi's wonderment. My duty as an artist, if I can call myself that, is to try to make the poems *a living lover, a living sage, a best friend.* I have referred to my work with Hafiz as *My Portrait of Hafiz*, and have posted a short essay with that title on the web. This book is part of *My Portrait of Rumi*, as I have two more books of his on the stove, I hope to someday complete.

I have used scholars' translations of Rumi as keys to open what I feel are other legitimate vistas and meaning within his poems. The greater the engagement, beauty, wit, and playfulness in his verse— the more one can walk away with—is to me, the greater the success and truth of the translation, rendering, version, *inspiration*, interpretation, or *portrait*.

A world treasure, a fascinating and vital life raft is Jalaluddin— one who is *still here/now and full of benevolence*. And who, with his love, can lift us from our mud holes when we are stuck. Then, when you are ready, he can ferry you out into the middle of the ocean, and, en route, strip you bare of everything but ecstatic gratitude. The encore starts in the midst of the splendor now seen. Existence starts pulsating with light (as it really always does) and welcomes you back into its arms. A divine breath rushes in, you gasp, you start choking on God, but cry out for more. What else is there now left to happen? I will tell you. A profound look of recognition comes into his eyes, of who, of who you really are. Rumi bows to your final journey, then tosses your butt into the sea. And in his compassion he leaves you there to drown and dissolve. Yes, my dear, drown and dissolve in your own Magnificently Sovereign, Luminous Being, which all, someday, will do.

—DANIEL LADINSKY
JULY 10, 2011

IF I HAD A SON OR DAUGHTER

I f I had a daughter or son in their teens, or even in their twenties, and I saw them holding a book titled *The Purity of Desire*, I might think or say to myself . . . *uh–oh.*

In wanting to balance this title and address what I feel is the very essence of this book—and what Rumi's life so extraordinarily exemplified—I would like to quote from a source I have come to greatly respect and trust in my own journey back home. I think this was the first piece of spiritual verse that I ever memorized. Somehow, now, I seem to know a few hundred poems by heart; they just became a part of me from holding them so close.

To me, Rumi and Hafiz, and all the great poets and saints, became what they were because they played this game so well, and via it, achieved a soul's potential.

THE GAME

To penetrate into the essence of all being and significance and to release the fragrance of that inner attainment for the guidance and benefit of others—by expressing in the world of forms, truth, love, purity, and beauty—this is the sole game which has intrinsic and absolute worth. All other happenings, incidents and attainments in themselves can have no lasting importance.

—MEHER BABA, from the book *Discourses*

The Purity
of
Desire

THE ASCENDING SOUL[*]

I died as mineral and became a plant, I died as plant
and rose to animal,

I died as creatures on hoofs and with feathers and look,
look . . . I became a beautiful woman, I became a
beautiful man.

What should we fear, darlings? When were we ever less
by dying?

Though, once again, I will know the demise of my senses
and thoughts, so as to mingle more with angel ways.

Yet, even from these heavenly realms we must pass on,
for all except God does perish.

When I have relinquished every aspect of self, I shall
become what the mind cannot conceive.

Oh, let me not exist in any form that is limited by *names*!
There is a divine *non-existence* that proclaims, in exquisite
organ tones,

*back to the source of the Immaculate we shall return, back
to the cause of every god . . . we are.*

---

* "The Ascending Soul," above, is rendered from the translation of Rumi which
appears in *God Speaks*, by Meher Baba (p. 33), as first published in 1955 by Dodd, Mead
& Co. The original translation, by Reynold A. Nicholson, appears in his book *Rumi: Poet
and Mystic*, published by George Allen & Unwin, Ltd., 1950.

THE BODY IS LIKE MARY

The body is like Mary, and each of us has a Jesus inside.
Who is not in labor, holy labor? Every creature is.

See the value of true art, when the earth or a soul is in
the mood to create beauty;

for the witness might then for a moment know, beyond
any doubt, God is really there within,

so innocently drawing life from us with Her umbilical
universe—infinite existence . . .

though also needing to be born. Yes, God also needs
to be born!

Birth from a hand's loving touch. Birth from a song,
from a dance, breathing life into this world.

The body is like Mary, and each of us, each of us has
a Christ within.

THE PROVINCES YOU EFFECT

Away from the city, where one need not be so on guard,
the beauty of giving to all around may again rise in you.

Our true nature is benevolence. One is just half one's self,
part of one's strength, a fraction of one's talents without
love's constant reign over the provinces you effect. Charity,
is it not clear, is an essential matter.

Even the earth is like an egg in my nest, and you, my mate.
This world needs our warmth against it, or things will perish.

There is a pristine stream in your field of vision. Seeing that,
you won't look thirsty, will not appear in want, or in need of
a cure—like the many.

Attention is rightfully given, turns to the person free of cares.
Only some kind of master, it is concluded, can extricate his
life from the maze.

Let it flow from your face—a knowledge. A shelter you then
will become in this turbulent part of space. From the summit
of laughter, reach down into time and stop it for someone else.
That would be such a blessing.

Open up a rare shop. Give competition to the finest brothels.
Let people catch something from your *heart* that will cause
no discomfort, but help them to sing.

You can find deposits of sounds of ancient truths once known,
that still are of tremendous value. If so, sell them way below
the great cost of your holy tears.

Away from the *city*, where you need not be so *on guard*,
you are more apt to realize . . . God tells a lot of jokes.

THE PRINCESS IS NAKED

Why should I seek? Why would God not let His right
hand touch something in His left that He cherishes?

We are the body His arms are attached to. And we are
the arms attached to Him, also.

Your misconceptions veil the holy. The Princess is naked
beneath the surface of every form. Your boredom would
vanish if you had more of a clue about the Reality I know.

Men and women, en route to their jobs, sometimes see
the Intricate Weave that sustains all—and never arrive
to punch the clock. The soul can then retire and may
wander out from the shadows.

Open your hand. If your Beloved refuses to reveal His
face there, to the extent that a tear of yours falls onto
His cheek, then begin to backtrack to the origin of your
life-line . . . the source of every self.

Start looking to the root of all this. Everything else we
do is really just a symptom of some miraculous illness
we caught, which can so impair one's vision and joy.

The Prince is naked, and in the mood for company,
beneath the surface of every surface.

When this becomes known, you will fall to your knees,
right next to mine.

WHO WOULDN'T BE PROUD OF THAT?

I relish good food. And I might relish even more
it then passing—*without any stubbornness*—the
next morning, easily from my big behind.

Once while traveling, I relieved myself in a field.
Gazing at it for a second, I thought . . . *golly, who
wouldn't be proud of that?*

I really did not need those flies to reaffirm my
opinion when they quickly gathered and then all
started to excitedly shout,

*Gold! We just discovered gold, a whole steaming
mountain of it!*

Nevertheless, I too can now exclaim, with equal
enthusiasm, at such a grand find, for I discover
a *vast treasure*—from God's being—that He
unloaded everywhere!!

AS SHAMS WAS TO ME

A sheep who had just lost her lamb was in grief, and the fullness of milk throbbed heavy within. And she prayed the best she could, in her sheep soul, for help.

Soon after that, she came across a lion cub, all alone and near dying. Although the scent of him triggered every warning in her,

her grief was so great to have a beloved near, and one who could bring release of the building pressure in her glands, that she lay down beside him.

And after a while, he began to suckle her, and they and God smiled in unison.

Strong, the young cub became, and he was accepted into the flock by most, always reflecting their traits. He even developed a passable *baa*.

About a year went by, when then a real lion came upon the herd, and saw one of his own eating grass and thinking it was a timid creature.

So the aged lion said to his kin, "Brother, what has happened to you, acting like that? You have completely identified with something you are not.

Come down to the lake with me, we will look into it together. It will be our mirror. You will see you are just like me, a great and powerful king."

Yes, that is the role of the Teacher, as Shams was to me—showing one *who they are*, so they can stop bleating, crying at night, and never again be afraid.

WHAT CAN THE OSTRICH KNOW?

Even if I am standing near to all, as I now forever will do,
what can the ostrich know of this remarkable bounty on
my face for all to enjoy, if its lovely, odd head is stuck in
a hole?

All my poems are about a lifting, so that you can see more
of God . . . of your own wondrous self.

I AM LOOKING FOR AN APPRENTICE

The scent of the rose garden reached you. Otherwise, you would have no knowledge of these words.

If you went to the house of a kind old woman whose pantry was full, welcoming she would be.

She might have you sit right before her, and with skilled eyes sum you up . . . to determine what could be your favorite of those things she could cook.

I am like that—someone with a marvelous wine cellar who loves to entertain, and who has a keen sense of what you most need.

It is so, Solomon was a wise ruler. There is a school both he and I attended.

Knowing what your own heart really wants, is knowing what everyone is really striving for. Compassion and kinship follow.

The way my feet respect each other and can work in a natural unison, I can now, with all.

If you can go a week and not belittle anyone in thought, word, or deed . . . let me know, for I am looking for an apprentice, an heir.

GREAT INTIMACY

It is like an exquisite spider web, this world, but I
don't get trapped.

I have ceased to tie the strings of one shoe to
another in the morning,

so now I don't trip over my wants. This leaves me
nimble. Any mountain I can scamper up.

A long rope shoved quickly into a sack can easily
get tangled and not be of proper use

when all of a sudden you need it. So I do everything,
everything with care.

It is like a miraculous weave of silk, the fabric of
this tender-looking sphere where we are camping,

but I don't get caught in any arms or lives, unless
they are loving, loving me.

Gazing at Her across a field some days, and desiring
great intimacy as we need, what can I do?

What can we do when God is acting coy, but to
be like a bird that sings to its mate?

THE PLUMS

They were expecting me, the plums. So when I
finally arrived, we picked up the conversation

exactly where we had left it about a week ago.

Plums talking? Why ever would you think they
couldn't?

What kind of nonsense must go on in someone's
head to deny them

such a sweet and sometimes useful ability—to
think and talk, and act at times . . .

just like us!

SUCKERED INTO A BAD DEAL

Real spirituality doesn't turn one into an *easy mark*. It will do just the opposite and make it less likely you ever get suckered into a bad deal.

Ninety percent of any depression you knew was probably due to things not going your way.

Or because the last time you did seem to have a choice, when you got back home with what you wanted,

it turned out to have more thorns in it than you expected—and maybe you are still picking some of those out.

As one nears light, intelligence increases. And that comes in handy, to step around the many landmines people lay.

And that comes in handy for what your heart most cares about . . . *love's frolic.*

TO MARVEL AT

Be like the wing on the way to the party
that can lift yourself and others.

Expectations, let them serve you, until the
present is always enough to marvel at.

A COIN TOSS FOR YOUR SOUL

I have seen it happen when a person dies: The soul will come to the gates of paradise,

and there, God will open a magnificent book and read a few notes His angels wrote beneath each name.

God reads that to see if the soul is worthy of entering His mind and heart forever.

And if God does not like what is written about one's life on earth, I have never seen Him sway from then saying,

"I think those angels of mine sometimes drink too much. They must have gotten you confused with someone else . . .

let's toss a coin to determine your eternity. Heads, you win, tails—*uh-oh*."

Once God asked me to polish that coin before He flipped it. I saw that both sides were heads. Yes, both sides were heads!

Guess that puts *uh-ohs* in their place . . . and a lot of other things tooooooooooooo!

A THIEF BOLDLY SAID TO THE JUDGE

A thief, standing before a judge, boldly said, "How can you punish me for any crime, when you know damn well all acts are decreed by God?"

To which the judge responded, "I do not dispute your theological insight, as I too come from a place of such refined thought and knowledge. But then, all I do is also destined.

So 20 lashes to your bare ass, by that strong man standing over there. Then for a month, whenever you sit, you might pray God decrees you *second thoughts* . . . about stealing bananas."

NO CONFLICT WITH ANYTHING I DO

God's face gradually fades from the infant's sight.
If this did not happen, you would never be able to
recognize and converse with the things you do.

A soul's blindness most always increases as the body
grows, and certain hungers set in, and one's attention
is turned that way.

Now that you have traveled so far and have seen so
much, what is it you most prize?

What pack horse does not feel relieved when its
burden is lifted? Desires, narrowed down, can do the
same, decrease the weight you carry, and unveil the
wonder in the present.

Just a single movement, a single impetus, I now have.
Thus, there is no conflict with anything I do.

What kind of man would ask his breath the reason
for its actions? Less demanding, questioning, I now
am of all I see.

God's face will gradually return to your perception. My
words will help draw back the curtain from your eyes.

A SHOP THAT GAVE FREE FOOD

I think I just want to be sad today, the way many
are in this world. True, God rides in my pocket,
as He does in yours.

Yes, I could lift Him out and look upon various
realms of light and know great happiness. Maybe
I will do that tomorrow.

The ocean has moods. Have you not seen how its
color can change, and the waves' force and heights
can differ?

When one gazes into me, sometimes I gaze back
the way a mirror usually does, with nothing too
surprising. That is, I let you see, reinforce, what
you thought you were.

Other times if you are close, another dimension
in me opens its arms and lets you in. Such an
embrace I can give, you might never return to
what you once called *self*.

A shop that gave away free food that tasted fantastic—
you can imagine the lines that would form in front
of its door.

There are creatures from other worlds in a queue
you cannot see, waiting to inhale, sniffing at me as
if I were the finest smelling dog in seven galaxies!

WHEREVER YOU SIT

Stars moving in other heavens, wanting to help those of faith—

if you lift up your skirt, you may catch one falling, as they sometimes do.

All in this world is inseparable from us. Time's duty is to prove that beyond a doubt. Once it does, nothing in any hourglass will ever move again in a way you would not want.

When you know your real status, no longer would you covet or borrow in any manner. All will even line up to pay you interest, envy thee, if you want.

Someday, wherever you sit will become a throne, and the four elements, your beautiful guards.

All your worries then will say goodbye. Moreover, they will never have existed.

THE PARTNER OF YOUR AFFECTION

I am a painter, a maker of the seen and the hidden.
Every day I shape sublime forms. And then, when
God comes to view them . . . they and I melt away
in Him.

Every phantom knows it lives in my kingdom, and
if I wanted, I could make anything vanish so easily
from any distance, like wax in a flame.

I am both mingled with all and also magnificently
sovereign. This dual state of being and not being
are tides . . . I let ebb and flow.

There is something to be said for anyone who sits
alone with dignity and silently begs for God.

I am the partner of every affection and act. I am
the only one who is truly guilty, and I am the most
innocent at the same time.

In once finding myself so desolate and empty without
the Beloved, He finally took pity on me and filled
me with *Itself*.

His *brush* and all His paints were then, of course,
mine. I now use them to draw a map to your self, so
you won't get lost.

THE SNOW LEOPARD

Left to its own ways, the snow leopard will not move
from its kill until it is satisfied.

I understand it may sound strange to speak of a lover
of God controlling Light,

the way a lion might a deer in its mouth, or the banks
of a river, the water,

and then, being able to store God in a safe place for
when one's divine hunger returns,

when the slightest desire ever arises again, to be
with Him.

Sweetpies, the reason most cannot touch Effulgence
at will—do with God as ever you may please, hold the
Infinite as tenderly as wished,

is because your thinking has cut short your reach,
does undermine your power,

because your beliefs of right and wrong have impaired
your spirit's needed agility for union.

Your and the world's images of God limit your knowing—that He always wants to play with you.

Most every classroom writes on the board what is not *most true* of love.

A saint is like a snow leopard, and God the prey the pir's heart constantly seeks to devour.[*]

For then, God will be forever inside, more alive than ever,

and the Beloved will never then leave you—in His true home, in your heart, as Shams is now always inside of me.[**]

There is a tollgate in my veins that could bring this world to a complete halt, if my every cell did not sing the word, Shams.

---

[*] pir, a Sufi expression of sainthood

[**] Shams-e Tabriz (c.1185–c.1248) was a Qutub, a Perfect Master. He possessed a raw grandeur and an independence that compelled him to wander and remain aloof from many. Much has been written about the relationship between Rumi and Shams, yet this tale, related by Meher Baba, is little known in their hagiography: Shams "used to play the game, chowkhat [similar to checkers], which was his favorite game. Rumi would invariably lose . . . After years with Shams, one day while playing the game, Rumi lost as usual and exclaimed, 'Alas! I have lost again!' 'No, this time you have won!' Shams replied. That very instant Rumi received God-Realization from Shams." (Kalchuri, *Lord Meher*, Vol. 18 p. 6055). (See also, *A Note on Divinity*, p. 109.)

WHERE THE SULTAN DRANK

From any well where the Sultan drinks, news spreads.

That place is then eyed differently. Women, given a
choice, may travel an extra distance to taste what he

has, and have that water slowly enter inside, while
maybe imagining some intimate aspect of moist
romance.

A man may find the ache in a malady has ceased,
standing where he was, using his sinew in like manner.

The Sultan drank from me. Tuned by His touch,
myths orbit my head. I become all's root.

An instrument in the market place I am, anyone can
now lift and play. For I can be as air on a scale, or the
sum weight of many earths.

Even movements from afar make me perform in a way
you cannot imagine.

My body is a puppet, and there is a string to me in
every hand. And I see all, likewise. I, the wind that
moves.

Why should it not be this way? I will lie down with
you, or dance, anytime you want. My soul, though, no

one can really know about, barely even me, realizing
now it is infinite.

A MAN ON A GALLOPING HORSE

A crazed man on a galloping horse, crazed with
thoughts of trinkets in the market and grudges
against others, even family and friends,

what will he see of the gardens all around, and
the miracle of his own hand?

What will he tell others of the wonder of his
steed, and the way their hearts beat in unison,
upon existence's drum?

How can he contemplate the earth's desire to
support a billion hoofs and millions of yearning
mouths, and never complain?

What kind of song could he write that others
will want to accompany?

What chances would he have to fall from his
saddle overwhelmed in gratitude?

TRY TO BE THE LEAST IN NEED

It is a person's duty to get oneself into a position where one can be generous with their time and silver.

Whenever you gather with friends or are in a crowd, try to be the one least in need. For simply doing that is giving.

But I want to express myself, my longings, and all my cares in human ways, some aspect of you might feel.

Who wants to deny you that, dear? I can listen to you from my seat on a chair, ever nearby, and see you as clearly as anyone has.

I am so close, next time you pass, I just might prove it and stick out my leg and trip you . . . let you fall into my lap.

OUR SOUNDS

They are like a lasting kiss, our sounds, when they are tender.

How else would I want to speak to you except in a way that unfolds your curves, rolls you out like a heirloom tapestry across a rare sky?

You have an important story to tell. It is like mine. Yours is nearly complete.

The last minute, though, is 1000 times more packed than all that has happened so far.

If you can soften your look on someone you have not been kind to for a while,

your power will increase, and in this world that is handy.

Who would not want the ability to say to sadness, *Be gone you rascal,* and have it respond—"Okay."

A LION SKILLFULLY PAINTED

A lion, skillfully painted on a large flag, may appear
so real it startles a young child who thinks he sees
a great beast leap.

But the lion's movement and apparent life are, of
course, wholly dependent on someone raising the
flag into the air, and the kindness of the wind, or
the carrier's purpose.

All of us, as it were, are remarkably sculpted on
some cloth-veil God hoists. We move in the current
of His breath, or upon the eternal wake He caused,
when He tossed a pebble into . . . *the Ocean of Being.*

And when the Divine ceases to caress, fuel and
impel our old desires, *as pure as they may have been,*
we move on;

we get raised higher. The limbs of the tree will
grow—I am talking about your consciousness, our
perceptions—and an even finer existence we will
taste!

The world will hear that from our lutes . . . about our
kingdom within, and the earth will come more near
to us for help, as my sweetness has drawn you.

THINGS ARE SUCH

Things are such, that someone lifting a cup,
or watching the rain, petting a dog,

or singing, just singing—could be doing as
much for this universe as anyone.

COME TO THEIR SENSES

With lightning coming from so many eyes
at times, what is one to do who can't escape,
but try and find a place that is safe to hide, until
those close come to their senses?

EACH TIME

There is not a flood in all the worlds
that can douse a sacred flame in me,
that builds, that rises even higher, each
time I slay another fear.

KNOWING YOUR GREAT ACCOMPLISHMENTS

Knowing of your great accomplishments, I am
proud to be with you—*you*, gazing upon these
words or hearing them.

Like that time you carried an ant you found in
your sack back two miles,

back to its nest, figuring it entered when you
lunched on a blanket, then napped beneath
that palm.

Was that not you? How do you know, when I
can see the future and all the kindnesses stored in
your soul just waiting to ripen and quietly give?

Yes, I am pleased with the work of your hands,
because your finest human acts few know, or that

is the way it will come to be. They are a good secret
to keep, our gifts, when you can. A mystical
awareness becomes more natural.

Creation needs someone who is truly humble
and cares about love. Otherwise, its walls would
all decay.

THE RESURRECTION TOOK PLACE IN YOU

The physics would not be different. The odds would not be less.

If one drops a clay pot from my roof onto a stone walk behind my house, unless something is there to catch it, it will always break. And any jewel inside will roll out, and could get hurt that way.

I know my students to be like this . . . each a perfect orb (egg) that requires such care, for they contain a treasure I do not want damaged. So, all the right love and warmth and shield, I am.

I hold a baton. If I touch it to your body, you will become conscious God is dancing within. A magnetic force will shift. Your vision will be so enhanced—in every possible detail—the truth will be revealed. The Christ's resurrection took place in your soul.

Are you ready for that awareness? Fasting might help remove the plug the outside world placed in your ear that obscures the divine voice. That will help lead you to all Knowing.

You are the body lying in any shrine. So, a pilgrimage to your feet, my poems have made.

I hold a baton existence carved. It wants to touch you. We should near.

WITHOUT A LOT OF HOOPLA

That conch shell you crawled into on land, then
grew so large in there, you got stuck—

I am going to help get you out. It is just a matter
now of whether I should use my hammer,

or chant some magic words that could knock
twenty pounds off your ego and/or waistline.

Then you could just slip back into God without
a lot of hoopla and sweat on both our parts.

Sorry though. I don't think there is any special
tonic, or voodoo, to remedy a plight quite like
yours.

So brace yourself, sweetheart. Here I come!

NEVER TOO BUSY TO CHAT

Seeing how many miles you have to go,
I set up a little stall on your route.

I serve a nice cup of tea, and I am never
too busy to chat.

WANDERING ABOUT THE HOUSE

I saw my Beloved wandering about the house.
He had taken up a lute and was playing a fine tune.

His melody attracted a lot of attention, as one might
suspect, and a wonderful chaos happened when He
began to sing.

My neighbor's cows and chickens jumped their fence
and crowded near.

Women ran from their bath houses, barely covered—
to that, I had no complaints.

Planets leaned down and began to take notes, and
otherwise stingy merchants started offering their goods
for half price.

When the Beautiful One has His wine pitcher in hand,
the rules of the universe bow, prejudices die, laws are
repealed, our jail time is cut short. People roll on the
ground laughing.

What are you waiting for? There are always great lovers
of God in this world . . . to party-hard with.

FLOAT ON YOUR BACK A WHILE

They come, those junctures, where it seems you
must *turn right* as opposed to making a *sharp left*.

Consequences from the *breeze*, from life, could
move you into a new city, relationship or frame
of mind.

Any notion of free will could be reinforced, from
your studying of maps, or *want ads*.

A leaf in the middle of a river, what can it do though,
if it gets an urge to go ashore and doze on the bank?

Maybe it could call out to someone working in
a field nearby? Maybe it could ask for help from a
passing boat?

So much calling we do to God, beseeching change.
And He might think,

*"Gosh, I just put you there—in a miraculous current,
in a world I think is hip. Try to have some fun. Float
on your back a while. Relax, look up at the stars!"*

LOVERS IN THEIR RIGHT MIND

Moments of happiness come to lovers in their right mind.

We may seem like two to the world's veiled vision, but we are one when our souls' ways meld in silence.

You know that; I am not telling you anything new. I am just chanting this refrain for my and the sky's enjoyment.

Look, the water of life comes from us. It can flow from our eyes so naturally, like a perennial spring that blesses the earth with its expanding, constant, nourishing embrace.

The thoughts of *you and I*—of difference—have dissolved in the beauty of being, in an emerald courtyard, ever present in the present.

We inspire the birds! Their songs are a lovely gossip we created. Anyone with warm blood in them cannot help but fall under a fine spell *our wings and sounds* cast.

And we should exploit any smitten by our charm, for their own good. The stars are on the lookout, hunting. They are searching for people like us, so why should we hide?

We should reveal our love and offer them something. Grant pointers and hints for everyone's vital pursuit of romance and connection.

And we will show them, why not, some wondrous, agile, perfected feats. We will invite any creature to spend the night with us, and of course, never charge any being seeking union with another form.

The thin crescent moon is your necklace now. It offers itself as adornment when the body completely unfastens itself, removes the stitches from every seam and boundary,

leaving only a radiant core behind that can ignite any wick that has gone out.

Go beyond the effects of idle or cruel speculation if it is ever aimed at you. An ant's ways, what can it do to alter the true majesty of our Himalayan nature?

Heaven will raise a toast to us. That is easy to say, for it does to everyone. It just can't stop; it knows we are God's royal heirs. But besides that . . . look at our great loveliness at every stage of evolution and inner glorious unfoldment!

A rare nutrient, laughter. Find a way to give us that, dear ones. It will waft between the poles. It will help balance all thoughts, acts, and tears.

For only one reason you labor, so that one day you and all can cease all labor,

and then just marvel, be astonished, at any object, movement or scent, finally recognizing—realizing—that there is nothing more you could possibly want than *what you have, right now.*

Moments of happiness, moments of happiness come to lovers, lovers in their right mind.

HELP ME FIGURE THIS OUT

It decided to remain at a precise distance from the
earth, the sun,

knowing if it came as close as it really wanted,
life as we know it would not survive and evolve the
way God wished.

There is a radiance in me I need to veil, keep in a
distant sky from most everyone, so that I do not
turn you into ash.

Nevertheless, I take birth every second. Also, I die
each moment. And our shoulders can bump, but
that does not mean you know me.

I have bought so many tickets into this world and
the next. The Conductor knows me so well, He
offered me His job.

Even though I go everywhere you do, I do not travel.

Help me figure this out, this paradox I live: I am
all movement, I am every act *and* profound stillness;
profound stillness, at the same time, we are.

Do you have any bright ideas about anything? I am
open to suggestions.

TAKE THIS FOR AN EXAMPLE

How does God resist us? I guess the way the
sun does the moon.

I mean have you ever seen him mount her in
public?

He appears to control his passions, but who
knows what happens during a full eclipse?
They might both squeal loudly.

All possibilities are on the table. Best we factor
that in.

Take this for an example: The next step you
take could trigger a trap door. You start to fall—
but upward,

for a second you feel like a comet whizzing
through the sky. God looks down, thinks
you are a bug, and grabs you in His beak.

And that then solves many things.

DON'T TELL ANYONE ABOUT THIS

Once Shams gave me a very embarrassing hat to wear
and told me not to remove it unless he pulled it from
my head.

Further, he said if anyone inquired about it, I was to
act like it was the most chic attire around and never
mention him being the culprit of *its source*.

You probably heard about that word "ego," and how it
roughs most up—keeps many fidgeting about all day
and obscures . . . *the gods dancing*.

But try this sometimes: if you aren't tough enough for
strange headgear, go somewhere where no one knows you,

dress like a bum, and don't bathe that day or comb your
hair. Walk around for hours muttering weird sounds;
become *unseated* from your norm. Though, don't go so
far a strait-jacket comes to hug you.

You have probably been glued too long to the same spot,
where light from another dimension cannot warm your
face.

There is a treasure map here for the clear-thinking mind,
and the brave.

BEYOND THE MOSQUE

God is all reason, and God brings all reason to naught.

In a peaceful classroom, in the cool shade of a garden,
I once intellectually agreed with this advanced
theological point: God is the slayer and God is also
the slain.

Some years passed, and war one day swept my land.
I heard women and children screaming from a field.

I ran to help and came across a bleeding, still pulsating
limb, just severed from a young body. I held this arm
to my forehead, and pleaded to God with all my might
to let this beautiful child again be whole.

And God said, "Why should I not sever from *Myself*
what I want and know is best? All is literally part of Me.
What of existence's perfection and all events therein
can any eyes know . . . until their mind and all one's
awareness is one with Me?"

God brings all reason to naught . . . en route to a divine
union. But who can bear His company beyond the
mosque, the church, and the temple's common view?

IN ANY OF MY MYRIAD FORMS

Who can I talk to but a yearning heart, when I am
whispering exquisite things about love?

How can you pay attention if your mind still shouts
within at events that happened years ago, or you
have one of your *guns* aimed at me, in any of my
myriad forms?

The earth's beauty is such that most have thrown
a net around all one can hold, and now they are
dragging *parts of her* up a steep hill.

Dear, who can blame you for wanting to possess
all the loveliness you can? But look what happens
when her moods shifts. You get kicked in the face
and then come to me pointing to your wounds.

Who can really listen but a yearning soul, when
I am whispering about the splendor of love?

A heart that has never been broken, what can it
really know about compassion and ministering to
others . . .

as you would me, if I fell from my horse, and came
to you, asking for help?

QUIET ENOUGH TO HEAR

You know about the holy, even if you won't admit
it. For how could that not be God, flowing through
your veins and sometimes whispering to you, when
you are quiet enough to hear?

You grew from a pot in His window. He watered
you every time that even a single cell of yours
spoke, *Lord I am thirsty, and my body needs to stretch
a bit more into the infinite, I think.*

A different kind of sun, one from a world with
ten times the seasons the earth knows, turned you
green and crimson and gold. You were magical!

But then you fell asleep and awoke so overgrown,
you forgot your great powers and felt fear.

Seeing from where you came and which direction
you are heading, it is a miracle to me, a miracle,
that you might think you ever did anything wrong.

When my neighbor's dog lost its toy, it began to look
around, confused and sad. But being a friend of God's,

I just reached into His pocket and found another. The
dog never told anyone about this, and I appreciated that.
But I thought I would let you know . . . how I can be.

TOGETHER THROUGH THE YEARS

It is for that moment when I might steady you so you
don't fall, I have added my blood to an inkwell.

Indelible now will be my mark on history's canvas and
upon any sincere debate of God where reason finally
prevails.

And when you have the strength, you too may find
another to hold up.

They lean against each other in a storm, those cypresses
grown tall together . . . through the years.

If they had not trusted and protected one another the
way they do, they would not have survived

and given us their grace and shade—a place for our
eyes to meet.

Our friendship can be like this: a needed lift, a sail,
a pillar, a springboard to taste the unfathomable.

It is to tend you as you come into being, like a new
world, that causes me to stay, gives me a purpose. Of
course I thank you for that . . . for letting me help.

A FIELD CAN BLOOM

Talking can be sweet. A field can bloom in your
eyes when sharing words with the right person.

An invisible effulgence wafts out from a heart
that is happy. That is an oxygen to us.

In some cities, smoke stacks pollute the air and
harm the lungs of many creatures.

A good song fills our chests too, but can have
the opposite effect—everything it touches
may be better off.

There is a governor of every region of space,
a divine agent; he or she may remain hidden,
but their business is your soul, as it is mine.

Words can fertilize space now and then; don't
deny yourself becoming enriched.

Find some ears that love the touch of your
sounds, and you theirs.

WON'T THREE OF US FIT?

These are like wedding vows, my poems, from me
to you—a sacred bond I take seriously.

What if you are already married, or partnered up, is
that a problem? Won't three of us fit in your bed?

It might stop some arguing if I was there. You could
blame me for stuff.

I have heard people say, "If there is a God why did
He let *this* happen—and *that* happen? And why do
crooks sometime seem to get off scot-free by not
getting caught?"

A fox trapped in a house with nothing to eat catches
sight of a rat that crawls into a hole in an expensive
pillow, and then tears it apart.

I am not sure if those last three lines have much to
do with this poem, or anything really. They just
popped in my head.

I thought I would just toss them into the mix here.
Maybe they are a code?

That idea of a threesome with you *on a cold night*
got me excited . . . and threw me off.

IN A VASE

Help her when her body's seasons begin to end.
Listen more as she transplants her ways to a time
of being more soft and reflective.

And then, with genders like me it could be said, as
the tally of the years mount, we need a different
caring, too.

With all the attention men once gave to that branch
that swung . . . *you know where*, and now has basically
retired,

that will cause some adjustments. But we will get it
all worked out.

Let's transplant our cares to a place in the meadow
where our efforts will still bloom,

and others will want to put what we have grown in
a welcoming vase.

SHOULD RING A TEMPLE BELL

If the word father or mother is spoken by a child,
a temple bell should ring with joy, but it often
doesn't. What happened?

On the contrary, it is troubling when so many
children on earth really wish their parents were
dead.

Something must have taken place in the womb.
Maybe some poison emotion seeped in, too often.

Or a face and sounds that cared for you once you
were born, just got too weird.

How to release that which is deeply amiss from
your mind?

Knowing pain can make kinder the hand and
tongue, do you think you can be more accepting
of the past?

The reed that has never been cut so deep, it then
weeps drops of its vitals . . . can it give us any
lasting music?

Let something ring your temple bell. Find that.
I know you can.

A VOICE THAT CALMS

A voice that calms, movements that calm,
eyes that quiet—dreams that also do the
same, and enliven too . . .

Be a precious donor of peace and hope.
Give love to all you meet,

for so many in this world are being torn
apart.

PLANNING A GREAT TRIP

There is nothing wrong in looking forward
to something.

Your heart might get excited and hit a better
stride.

More color could come to your cheeks, and
you might even . . . *meet someone there!*

With all this talk of being present in some
spiritual dens, don't let that deter you from

planning a great trip.

EVEN IF YOU WERE A SEX ADDICT

I might have to slap my pencil a couple of times
if it does not stop writing titles like this.

Here is a matter for consideration, though: even
if you were a sex addict, and I was sketching lovely
nudes,

aren't there only so many you could look at, before
you got fidgety and wanted to do something else?

Any work a person does becomes a kind of display
window in the world's shop.

With so many things vying for your attention, one
has to be clever to get you to come by, walk in.

Sex sells, I hear. Guess I am trying to cash in a
bit and yes . . . get your *attention.*

ONE DAY I CONCLUDED

Water says to thirst, "I am over here." A roasting
hen, thinking along the same lines, passes a note
to someone's hunger which reads,

"No need for an empty ache in your tummy or
heart, *try me* . . . I have a great reputation."

Beauty in nature, which is usually within walking
distance or your vision's reach, rarely charges a
a thing to combat loneliness

and often says, "Put your spirit's arms around me,
you will feel better."

One day I concluded . . . *Why resist all this sweet
talk?* And have been better off ever since!

GET YOUR ASS AWAY FROM ME

When the trouble comes, and it will, *O yeah*,
I hatch a plan. I start a strategic, wise defense

that first involves: I try to learn from it. I may
keep my gripes silent, and rarely a wince will
appear in my eyes,

but I am just waiting for my moment of leverage
to then say, *Now get your ass away from me.*

WHO IS LEFT STANDING?

On this battlefield we have entered, who
is left standing? It is the woman and man
of integrity.

On this battlefield where we have come,
who is left to tell the tale as it should be
told? It is the woman and man of prayer.

YOUR CHARMS MAY QUADRUPLE

Being a guest in the universe's house, why not go
out and greet it sometimes in the early morning,

when it may seem *she* is just waking up and is in
a soft mood and may appreciate more our special
thanks and admiration? We may win her favor and
get a kiss.

Embrace all you can between the poles. Enriched,
then, will be your day, better your luck, more
eloquent your gestures. Your charms may quadruple.

Who wouldn't want that? My suggestions seem a
smart move.

And the jewelry the sky wears at night—might as
well say hello to that, if you are feeling cordial.
Your evening might become filled with intrigue.

Invisible spices are falling from heaven all the time.
If your eye is not holding its hand out, or your
mouth or heart not open,

how will you ever get a full taste of something
that will cure you of many things?

EMPTY IT OUT IN FRONT OF ME

There have been thousands of things for you to
pick from to put in your backpack on this journey.

But empty it out in front of me, if you cannot look
in all directions and nothing bothers you.

I say that because, if what you are working with—
what you are carrying everywhere you go—has
not brought you peace,

would it not, my dear, then make great sense, to
try something I might offer?

INDIVIDUALISTIC

There are a myriad different sounds in this world
and in other dimensions.

And does not each human voice have its own
fingerprint?

How could so many things come from the
same womb of One Being and still appear so
individualistic?

How could the effulgence of God ever be
diminished, hidden in any single object to the
extent we could look at it and not squint, or not
call it beautiful?

It was so that you might have company at every
stage of your blindness becoming cured. The
surgeon's patch is best removed gently, so that
no damage is done to your usefulness to us.

Follow though, back to the core, anything with
a name until all concepts disappear, until you
come to that place again where there is just You,
the source of the Source of all madness and
sanity profound.

SWAT TEAM

I was feeling a little down one morning,
so down—I had to call in the swat team.

Luckily, they were close . . . those bluebirds
and rabbits and squirrels.

THOUSANDS OF YEARS OF FOREPLAY

It used to work this way: you tidied up a bit,
maybe even a lot, before meeting a person you
hoped to have some kind of an alliance with.

Trust and respect were a key component. Once
you had that on ice . . . business could be discussed,
or *some arrangement* could be made, for a night
together.

But now it just seems anything goes. Most everyone
wants to get right to it . . .

everyone but God. For it appears obvious, He is
still into thousands of years of foreplay.

I mean, you have heard of reincarnation? And
know something about *dry spells* before the Big
Bang happens again, *in a kind of reverse?*

You return from where you came.

THE SEVEN PILLARS OF RUMI*

Be like the river that breaks out of its confining mold and floods upon our needs and longings—with generosity.

Learn the ways of the day candle (the sun) that has concluded everyone deserves its light, which when felt deeply will bring about the conception, the growth, of spirit's abundance and harmony in us.

Starve your tongue of any sounds that demean another. Let your eyes be as the night that can conceal so much of what the day heard. Please, allow your face to show us your soul's peace and beauty.

If anger or greed or prejudice rises in you, practice being a corpse, and your moments of elation and feelings of gratitude will increase many fold.

There are wealthy gods wanting to die every hour. They are looking for heirs to carry on their work in time and space. Humility, my darling, will help reveal a pricelessness they (the Great ones) and the earth and sky want to impart into your dance.

The rose bud is destined to open and the jewel to be found with my gaze upon it, as it is upon you. Still, worry will come at times. Whenever you fear anything, hold my hand tighter.

Free of any agenda but love, how simple, how exquisite, how full all, all, has become. Look, the infinite silence and infinite distance between the words on this page want to swallow me now; the Divine is hungry. I will let it; though I might return again, just in case you need me.

---

* Based on "Seven Advices of Mevlana (Rumi)," which is greatly popular in modern-day Turkey.

PICK THE LOCK

Being in a hurry throws the key on the ground
to a door I want you to enter.

If you read my words slowly and out loud, they
will help to pick the lock.

THE CHINA DOLL IN US

Some people punch a hole in your being whenever they are around, and then you leak out energy and other kinds of vitals you could have used.

Then, there are people who can connect you to a depth in their heart and for a moment, maybe an hour, maybe a day, you will share their radiance.

The china doll in us, at some point, will no longer break. It is then you will find you have the ability to heal others, in a way few in this world can.

A RARE BREAD IN EGYPT

My verse resembles a rare bread in Egypt.
Nights can pass over it, but still it will be so
nourishing and fresh.

Many kinds of birds could come and peck at
me, and carry my remains into the sky.

Wonderful, some pieces will then fall all over
this earth.

And living seeds will take root in any heart
that holds Rumi close, or can swallow what
I say without a big belch.

My words resemble a rare dish in Damascus,
many days can greet them, but still they will
remain so fresh.

SHIT! WHAT HAPPENED?

Unless it is on drugs, or certifiably crazy, the fish
squirming on the hook should say,

Shit! What happened?

And then maybe, just maybe, even do something
clever about it—the way we should.

WORTHY OF A TATTOO, ANYWHERE

I think there should be some kind of a checkpoint
in books, in the classics anyway, to make sure you
are actually learning something. To make sure you're
not goofing off again, or just toting a fancy title
around to help you get laid.

Some gate could come down around you at random
pages. Some guard should come out and make you
recite a few lines from memory, or at least have you
discuss a few points with intelligence.

Like putting honey or milk in your coffee or tea, the
flavor becomes different, you grin more, drinking it.

Good verse will do that to your mind, if you let it
soak in. It could turn you into a fine store where
tourists will come and locals hang out.

And while on this subject of sexual stuff and wanting
to keep it to just a few pages in this book, here is an
eloquent truth most mullahs withhold, but is worthy
of a tattoo, anywhere:

*As souls and bodies make love with each other; so will
God, with you.*

I COULD SAY YOU ARE
TRESPASSING RIGHT NOW

I am a border you need to cross. I am vast, though,
you will need my help.

How many days would it take to travel just across
my palm if I showed you its real size?

I am a limb the universe has built a nest on. Any
prayer for rain or help comes to me.

Bow to the two poles and then to the place where
light shows us its tenderness each day, and its power.

Now to the West, be so kind to lower your head,
and offer a look without a stone in it ready to fly,
to your neighbors there.

Unite with all, so the world's beauty increases, does
not wane.

I could say you are trespassing right now, wherever
you stand. But I am not like that. I would never press
charges against you, for anything.

The one who owns the joint, you should go meet
Him. He gets drunk sometimes and starts giving
away royal titles, presidencies, palaces, heavens, earths.

BETWEEN YOU AND THE STREET

Falling the way you do at times, I offer my body
between you and the street.

Any concern for you from another heart, protects.
Prayers can solicit angels' help.

What is meant to be, is just that, and will unfold.

Still, show some guts. Say to destiny, "I am calling
the shots around here; take a hike."

That probably won't change much, but you will
get my respect.

Falling the way you will at times, I offer my body
between you and any street, pothole, or abyss.

WHERE NOTHING NEEDS REPAIRS

Someone might pet you more if you did not twitch
or scratch so often as if you had fleas, mange, or some
psychotic illness.

If you put in a few hours in the wild, alone, nurturing
your inner sensibilities, and sat cross-legged like a yogi,
your hygiene might improve 360 degrees and word
would spread.

What sane person does not want their popularity to
increase? Some want fame to exploit; others want that
so they can give more. Both are a sacrifice.

Stop acting like you are on a budget when it comes to
love. Why fuss so much with what will not be here in
a hundred years?

Free yourself up, dear. Next time it seems you have a
choice to build something on earth—and then have
to guard the damn thing,

or wander off in heaven where nothing needs repairs,
take the latter, the way any lazy wise man would.

WHAT ISN'T BOOBY TRAPPED?

What isn't booby trapped to explode if you don't handle it just right? Especially any matters of romance with a modern-day earthling.

WE EXCHANGED RINGS

Wonder and I took a vow; we exchanged rings.
I fell in love, and she accepted all my desires.

I am lying now in a meadow, holding the sky
in my arms.

If I turn my gaze away from you, this earth,
please do not feel ignored. I'll come back and
kiss you again.

BETTERMENT OF ALL BETTERMENTS

If God just showed us His funny-face more,
by putting His thumbs in His ears and then

wiggling His fingers and hands, things would
be a lot different down here. I am certain.

And for betterment of all betterments. Yep.

Yep, indeed.

Thus, my close ones see me do that now and
then!

THE BEAUTIFUL FACE

We just naturally turn toward her loveliness.

The clouds may gather in the sky in a graceful
manner that lifts our gaze to them.

Something we see there may touch us for a
few moments in a way we so needed.

Words in a poem can be like this: causing
formations, images in your mind, that can
create chemical synergies,

that so elevate vision—the single eye gets
ignited,

and the light, *the beautiful face, the exquisite
One*, that was hidden, is revealed.

MOUNT SINAI

Cleanliness and being well-mannered would make
you *suspect* in some circles I travel in.

Clothes that aren't soiled and smell too sweet,
what do they know about rolling around on the
ground in ecstasy?

Love inspired Mount Sinai to become a pillar
capable of holding up the impetus of all desire.

You have seen how a carpet is beaten to remove
the dirt.

Go to someone who has the power to hold you
upside-down, or turn you inside-out, and club

all your hidden arrogance to death. That will help
your sadness to die.

IF SOMEONE TENDS US

If someone tends us, we will be like the orchard that reflects a summer's perfect . . . gold turn. We can become wonderfully burdened with many kinds of fruit from the nutrients of others' love,

asking then only to be harvested, given away or kept close. If someone properly cares for us, we will fill baskets with what God Himself eats. Otherwise, our talents may feel lost and cry.

When all that has come from His mouth, *existence* can be seen as immaculate and at last integrated into our vast system of being, you will stand out amongst us, and I will be the first to cheer.

Like an emperor who starts giving away all his wealth because he has found God in his heart, I have become. I am like rain now, you can just lie there like the earth. I will not judge your merit. I will intimately touch you because you're in need.

Effort is not required. Any kind of doing might get confused with virtue or vice, which my abundance has no concerns of whatsoever. Just open your legs, smile invitingly. Is that asking too much? Forcing myself upon anyone, I never do.

Our romance has begun. That is what is happening now. My every word is courting you, and you, simply being here, are blessing me with encouragement.

The quieter you become, the more our souls will know they are the same. I like the way this is going. There will be only one of us soon. For when we tend the beautiful, the beautiful, the Divine Orchard we will find.

THEIR SECRET WAS

A married couple used to come see me once in
a while. Among the many I knew who were wed,
they appeared the most happy.

One day I said to them, "What marital advice
could you offer to others that might help them
achieve the grace you found?"

And the young woman blushed and so did her
husband; so I did not press them to answer.
But I knew.

Their secret was this: That once every day, for
an hour, they treated each other as if they were
gods and would, with all their heart, do anything,
anything, their beloved desired.

Sometimes that just meant holding hands and
walking in a forest that renewed their souls.

IN PLACES YOU CAN'T REACH

You might have noticed how animals may
groom each other in places that they cannot
reach on their own. That is what my poems
are all about.

What a deal!

THE MAYOR AND HIS WIFE

Only late at night, when all the kids are in bed,
might God come to earth and speak frankly with

His most elite students, saying something so few
really want to hear or could live, for that *tune* goes:

"Run from any situation that might turn profitable.
If someone praises you, spit in their face.

If for a moment you feel secure, find somewhere
to live where you are terrified.

If somehow you have the great misfortune to win
a fancy award for being brilliant or wise, put an
end to that foolishness ...

simply take off all your clothes, and try to kiss the
mayor or his wife.

Yes. The cops will then just haul you away!"

MOVE CLOSER TO THE RIVER

The prairie's ablaze, and all the birds and animals move closer to the river, following their knowing.

God's breath whips the fury even higher, but the lone tree on the plain cannot leave.

It quickly calculates its fate, while eons of dignity from all the forests that have ever been now step forward in its heart to help . . . to lend their courage.

It understands this rising conversation, this potential brilliant-glowing, fatal end. See, it folds its leaves in prayer and begins to sway and dance!

See, how given no other choice, it now even invites the annihilation of its self, knowing life is too sacred to ever end, knowing all is just another beginning.

The Sky can never deny such bravery, defiant-charm, and grace. And the tree does so with no expectations at all. For so naturally inherent in it—and us— is sublime poise.

Weak-kneed now becomes the King before one of his subjects, for something just mirrored Him—rivaled God's strength and beauty.

So rightfully weak-kneed and humbled becomes the Lord before such fearlessness and love . . . *He starts carrying buckets from the well.*

DRAG ME ACROSS THE SKY

I said to my Lord, "Never be shy, dear, for you are always welcome to use the perfected instincts of the emerald falcon, whom God taught to hunt so well."

Light's talons, I invite you to deeply pierce my being with mortal wounds. Love, love, tear me to shreds, for will I ever feel complete until you do?

Drag me across the sky, sweetheart; let the world look up and point at me. Having their attention, I might drop useful hints in poems that may comfort their minds and guide the eye from sadness.

Yes, a thousand times indeed—overpower me with your stunning ways and manner. Your politeness—not around me, nor your shyness, as I have already discussed.

Just drag me across the heavens without any reservation. Uproot, vanquish, all I have understood, for cannot you see I am your begging, willing, longing prey, and all I do . . . a fetter?

If you do not let me fall at your feet and die in ecstasy, you keep me from my fate. Cruelty, then, any court could rightfully accuse you of, and who would want a reputation of being mean?

What kind of strange, weird people would you then attract? So let it happen, the lover's blessed destiny: the union of death, the holy demise to there being anything, anything, but You.

This sacred passing—and therein true knowledge—is discovering the hand can touch only God, the limb can only sway against His luminous thigh.

Every kiss God has felt upon His lips and body. No wonder, no wonder, He smiles so often.

A BABY MONKEY

In a jungle this thick, it's hard to perceive very far.
Strange news, noise, and scents can reach one, that
cause scare, pain, worry and doubt.

The atheist is like a baby monkey, who can suffer
many ills, in being separate from the Truth, in
feeling distant from the *Mother.*

Though if anyone were to climb to the top of a
mountain tree, and see unobstructed, in every
direction, what was really happening—what really
always Was . . .

God would be the certainty of certainties! And the
earth's grandeur—and all occurrence would admit

they hung from the hem of His robe, over an eternal,
effulgent sea, where one day they will *let go of all* and
drown—more happy than they have ever been.

LOVERS TOUCHING

To my eyes, lovers touching are folded wings
in a beautiful prayer.

But yes, what heights and great expanse one
can also reach

when tenderness is placed upon the bow, and
our spirits know no gravity.

WE STARTED OFF PURE GOLD

We started off pure gold. Then people began
polluting us when we were too young to fight
back.

If a jeweler now examined you he might exclaim,
"What happened? You turned into pyrite!"

Don't be worried by such a candid remark; don't
let it depress you, for there is a way

to reverse this process. Everything I write gives
practical *clues, clues, clues!*

A SMART PRAYER

A smart prayer is like a good scout, an expert tracker,

who finds God's campsite and bootlegging still.

THE CAMEL WAKES

The camel wakes after long journeying and many nights
of short sleep and thirst.

Today the master does not load her with heavy sacks, nor
will she feel the bite of his whip.

He gently leads her to the meadow where the caravan is all
gathered in the pink light of dawn.

He drops the harness that has reined in her spirit. Instantly,
she gazes in awe and sublime gratitude at a cool stream
and eternal lush field . . . *she becomes.*

Yes, she becomes everything around her, the way a soul
does at union.

Profound thanks she nods, as names and forms dissolve.
Thanks for everything, as her heart embraces the tiny,
miraculous stitch in existence—this earth and every object
really is.

Wild roses and carnations run to greet her, trees and hills
bow in her direction. Clouds lean down and tickle her chin,
hoping she will reciprocate—*with laughing ease.*

Who can resist paying homage to such awareness and
strength, for her whole body now—like the sun—is
pouring *life* into this world.

The camel rises, wakes forever, forever, after long journeying
and many hard nights of tears.

STRANGE HOW MY POWERS INCREASE

Most everyone, all day long, says and acts, "I am,
I surely am."

I wonder what happened to me, for all day long I
hum, "*I am nothing*, I am the personification of some
glorious nil."

Strange, how my powers increase the less I become.
Every step I take toward complete effacement, look
what takes place . . . my radiance grows,

and more gather to receive it, as the dark side of the
earth turns to the morning light it craves.

Standing in a line, if someone butts in front of me—
my immediate response: I am so happy to see them.

If I am at a fancy dinner and someone spills food on
me . . . my clothes know they could not be better
off, and I smile.

One night, I found myself at a conference the stars
were having. Enjoying being nothing, I had zilch
to say.

God takes notice of people like me and then sends
someone like Shams along to rough us up, and pour
into *our cup* . . . a divine task. Maybe it is my poems,
the way they can amuse and kiss.

THE AVALANCHE OF WINGS

As much as You breathe into my heart, so does it rise and
exhale resplendence.

You did the same thing to the earth, so kindly let it know
Your touch . . . the way Your bride must, so many times.

It then had no other choice but to increase its bounty,
pregnant as it was. Look now at its enormous ability

to shelter the myriad creatures, letting them dance, play
and raise their families against her breasts' *seasons*.

So fertile is Your eye's gaze, that you plant into whatever
You behold . . . Your own divine self.

And *all* You see! Can you begin to calculate that meaning?
When you do, half your burden will dry up.

Every soul is heir to the Crown. That is the promise in
Your face. Any who have neared You have *seen*, know.
Yes, for certain.

As much as You breathed into us, that much we became.
And now, now, all that Your being has ever experienced,
shall everyone.

We need to roost on the formless again so that we no
longer feel limitation's torture.

We have circled love for eons. Beloved, just lift your falcon's
drum, and we will return; not even one note we need to
hear. Simply beckon us with a wink.

The avalanche of wings, the avalanche of wings, please cause!

LET SOMEONE SOBER WORRY ABOUT THAT

It is not easy to find the grace that makes an *extreme*
lover of God the way they are. So free.

They can go unwashed, act disgraceful and scream;
they can care nothing about a raise in pay or getting
fired.

Is that the way you want to become? What might
happen to all that respect you once craved?

But sometimes they burn with a passion you dream
of. Sometimes their mind knows a peace you may
have not thought possible.

How long will you care for the distracting litter of
this world and collect it, like a garbage man?

Watch out, dear. Serving greed for only a second will
put your life tighter into a cage.

Let someone sober worry about things going badly.
There is more for us to do—

like looking at that branch's hand move against the
sky's private regions, and seeing her become so alive.

THE WHOLE PLACE IS A MAN-EATER

This whole place is a man-eater. The equator is
the axis of its jaws.

This beast is so large, most have no idea it really
exists,

just as a minnow judging the size of the ocean
doesn't have a clue.

Worse yet, the beast has powers and has cast
such a spell over most,

that people willingly bring themselves to some
favorite spots where the beast likes to relieve
itself,

rather than at least wait until the monster hunts
them down, and indeed it will at some point.

One of these favorite spots to defecate is anywhere
politicians might lounge about and divvy up what

they stole from us. So watch out there.

BE LIKE THE CAT

Be like the cat, so alive after the mouse,
never wondering or questioning why,

when there is really only God, only God . . .
touching our

paws.

TO HELP THE VILLAGE SURVIVE

Any heart that has slept close to God for one night,
the world may wisely become leery about,

knowing that soul is now capable of almost anything.
A *specialist in erratic behavior* is sometimes a lover's
trademark.

For who has ever bucked heads with the Infinite and
then not have appeared on tilt at times?

But fight any tendencies to appear odd or ever say,
the hell with everything . . . for it is only a dumb dream.

Yes, please, don't think like that, for even *imagination*
is sacred, and we have valuable work to do—

like women working in the fields and grinding the grain
from the harvest

and carrying heavy jugs of water on their heads to help
the village survive.

Any heart that neared God for one minute, the world
would be wise to honor.

GIVE HIS EARS A RUB

When the old drunkard on his donkey cried out,
"Where is my ass? I've lost her again!" those
standing near had a good chuckle . . . seeing he
was upon it.

The Beloved too must have a belly laugh, as we
madly search for Love, which we *straddle* all day,
and sometimes all night.

The omnipresent never says, "I am over here, but
not over there." Surely, that has to be the case.
It has no prejudice.

The translation of that is simple: Wherever you
are . . . *give God's furry ears a rub.*

THE ROSE IS AFRAID OF WINTER

The rose is afraid of winter in the part of the world where I live.

I should not have to explain to you why, for I bet you are bright. If need be, a little puzzle is fun at times to jimmy with.

Beware of those affections that make you susceptible to ruin. Who would invest all their savings with a strange man just passing through your town?

Look how an orchard can appear so beautiful, even knowing a frost may soon come to destroy its blossoms. But your beauty, dear—each pilgrim, will never fade to me.

I think I am going to start giving you some kind of a test, after you close this book. I have mentioned a thought like that before, so it must be a good idea.

A doctor learns skills you hope he will remember, if he is cutting you open with a knife.

Yes, I think I should devise a quiz . . . to discover any useful points you have gleaned from what I taught.

There are things you already have in your closet that you are shopping for again, around me. If you can sit still long enough, my dear, the memory of them will return.

The ultimate uselessness of a teacher is part of my lesson for you.

THE BOTTOM LINE OF POETRY

Once when I was asked these two big questions,

What is the bottom line of poetry? What is its goal?

I responded, *I know that. Do you really want to . . . be in the loop, though?*

And the person said, *Yep!* So I gave them the truth, no holds barred, as if I were talking to an old drinking buddy—and not needing to mince words:

It gets you into a position . . . where you don't want to move an inch.

You know what I am talking about? You aren't a prude are you?

I didn't think so. Or how would you have gotten so far in this book?

HELL, I AM ALL OVER THE PLACE

I travel with every caravan without ever leaving my
house. And our intimacy, I so cherish; all food is me,
touching your lips.

I am hatched every second, but I am also the egg,
waiting to unite with sperm in a billion wombs.
The grass in the nest, that is me, too.

And any forest, I grafted it there, it came from a
region of my soul that is hard to believe.

Which leads me to this truth: *Hell, I am all over
the place.*

I am now the greatest champion of all art and all
acts, because I cannot cease to applaud.

I am the connoisseur of everything, and developed
this useful trait: I taste wine all day but still I am
sober. So much so, the affairs of the universe all
seek my advice.

The clouds, when they are feeling shy, sometimes
need me to coax them to rain.

And rivers run into my arms because they are always
open, and I am so wide.

No one is at a distance from me; I like having you
so close. I could be a great spy in any war, but I have
other things I would rather fool around with.

Not one tear have you shed that I have not counted
and worshipped. And for every one of those I am in
debt to you. When would you like me to pay?

I am weeping now, myself, because love just entered
this poem from an angle that caught me off guard.

How can it be, that even in infinite knowing there
are surprises? I guess so God doesn't get bored!

In wanting to keep things simple, if a friend ever
asked you to sum Rumi up, you could just say,
Hell, he is all over the place.

There is something my eye bestows to all I look
upon, that will help you to become like me—

all over the . . .

ONCE BEFORE YOU DIE

At least once before you die, be like a candle that stands
up and burns throughout a whole night in prayer,
keeping a vigil, as you would, if the Prophet appeared
in the room where you live.

There is a devotion I have found that can make God
so intimately close, I can count the hairs on His chest
when He opens His robe.

There are so many nights to sleep. Surrender one, if
you can. In the most quiet hours, the White Bird sings.

Beseech for a full day, in your heart, the inner kingdom.
Do what you can, my loves, to remove the veil that
keeps you . . . suffering want.

YOUR BREATH UPON ME*

Those precious words of hope that entered this world from
our souls,

heaven saw them. They were not allowed to die. They were
too giving and beautiful.

Love is not a singular event in the luminous dome or upon
this radiant earth

that can rise or fall like a comet and is then never *seen again* . . .
or rarely talked about.

For when a heart is most in need, we will come back. We
will caress any face that turns in our direction. We will want
them to join us. Join us!

All the promises of God shall come true, as they did for me.

Soft whispers and laughs often contain more truth than anything
the world might call—serious, important or real.

Having said so much, I should be quiet and see how close
you always are.

But O, look what just happened! Your breath upon me now
makes me sing one more time:

*Those exquisite words of hope and giving heaven spoke through
our sublime union—will never be allowed to die.*

---

* Some believe there was a "Last Letter of Rumi" sent to his teacher, Shams. What I have
gleaned from different versions, tales, myths of this "letter" and from what I believe about that
subject myself—and their astounding relationship—the above verse was crafted.

A'ISHAH

I once heard that when the Prophet Muhammad
was among us, at times, to comfort his feelings, he
would ask A'ishah, his youngest wife, to come to his
private room.

And when she came, with eyes no one could describe,
and with a touch paradise gave her to serve him,

when their faces were close, having waited all her life . . .
as it were—between the times their hands and breath
knew each other's eternal completeness, forever giving,

she would sit so near him, and Muhammad would
whisper, "My darling, let your soul turn to music
that all creation will hear when it enters me.

Sing for us a song of great tenderness that all beings
and forms in all time will feel against their hearts, as
my heart *holds it, sacred.*

Sing for the earth and sky my being tends. They
need you now. I want you, my divine self, my divine
self, to sing of love."

THE MILL HAS NO GRUDGE

We are like grain and life, the mill. The *mill* has no grudge. The moving stone never wishes us harm.

It just does its job of making *all* more digestible and consummate.

When you have become golden in the fields from swaying with light,

the sickle moon will turn its gaze in your direction and harvest you some holy day.

Then his attendants will put you in sacks, and from ports the Ocean made, you might travel around the globe, offering alms.

Word will spread how someone grew from His body, and we will come to feast.

Leaving the table after an hour's normal meal, hunger can still be there. Because—yes, there are other foods we so require.

Real learning will help you figure things out. Like the next time you hear I am town,

you will quickly conclude . . . I should go visit that that old guy.

IN OUR OWN BACKYARD

There is a golden bird living on the side of a cliff.
We have become friends.

It is very large; its wings can stretch such a vast
distance, there is nowhere it cannot go.

I would not ask you to turn my way, listen to my
words, or bring me anything,

if I could not offer something you want, like a
ride on its back with me.

Holding my hand in mid-air, you can lean over
any world, and see wonders you never thought
existed.

Why should we not play like that sometimes,
having fun, exploring some nooks . . . *in our
own backyard.*

I WOULD GIVE MY LIFE FOR THIS

I would give my life for this: for one line of verse so rich, and full of salvation, thousands would remember it as if it were their own name.

And if they, or a cherished one, were ever in trouble, on the verge of collapse from loneliness, grief or despair, they could just recite it with whatever strength they had left.

Then God, no matter how shy He was feeling that day, would reveal Himself, for at least a moment, and that would be all that was needed—a second of truly seeing Him,

which is the most many in this life might come to know. He might even tickle you then, just to make certain He wasn't a mirage, and on a spot that would surely alter your mood.

Would not that be all that was needed for one to gain some courage and take a stand and move on with some zest?

Yes, a line so exquisite it would be passed from eye to eye, hand to hand, flute to drum, generation to generation, language to language, speech to song.

Thankfulness . . . falling to your knees. Maybe, something I already wrote with Shams' pen contains light from that Sun that will forever yield His comforting scent,

bring about such insight, you too will discover . . . your own holiness. Yes! I would trade my life for that, for one line of verse so beautiful, so beautiful and giving.

WHEN NAMES WERE NOT

I loaned existence its being, for I was there on that day when names were not.

Creation had no need to pray until I frightened it . . . by taking one step back—desiring my formless self again.

Seeing me about to disappear the world gasped with all its heart, saying, "Don't leave! Please, don't leave."

So God and I agreed to be the root of every form and act, and nurture all within our understanding and our eternal presence.

I saw the perfect rose upon the cross.* A drop of holy oil it bled, so that you can anoint your inner eye and bring an end to your suffering.

A merchant as rich as I, should not be able to travel about unmolested.

Don't sit there acting reverent or polite. Ransack my body and my words. Because I was there on that day when there was no time or space.

I loaned each soul love. I minted every religion, every phrase, every coin.

I showed these words to God and He sang, *There is no fantasy in what Rumi says.*

---

* *the perfect rose: Jesus*

IF YOU ARE EVER IN NEED

If you are ever in need of a kiss, bring to mind
the smell of fresh bread

and taste again a touch you once loved or are
hoping for.

Feel the firmament lifting you in its arms—well,
well, at least pretend it can, and one day it just might.

And was there not some moment in meditation
where light once bathed you and surely could
again?

Bring to mind the smell of fresh bread. That
aroma surrounded Shams at times, and I drank it in.

It has now formed an oasis, where to gather,
around my every pore.

WHERE I AM PLACING YOU

God is glad to be forgotten when you are happy,
because everything He has worked for is then
coming true, if a divine independence you can
sense.

An important goal is reached when you laugh.
Any fiddling or exertion with spiritual thoughts
you can let rest when you are respectful of others.

But you may still become tied in knots from the
spinning currents all around. If this were not the
case, you and I would be one,

and your joy would feed the atoms. Then the world
would migrate to your side, wanting to tend your
behest in love's service; in love's service of the Throne,
where I am—I am placing you.

FLY HEAVENWARD DEAR

Fly heavenward, dear. Let your wings unfurl to their full expanse.

Gather from the sky's fields and intimate regions that rare, unalloyed quality and light.

Bring it back to your nest. Weave it into your eyes, sounds, movements and touch.

Then invite all of us over to your house, if you are willing, if you are willing . . . to let us stay.

NOW CLOSE THE BOOK

All that you have read should help close every book.
Any page you have ever turned should have aided in
dusting off—rending—the veil over your glorious eye.

All talk and words are foreplay. I have other things
in mind for us now.

A NOTE ON DIVINITY*

Poetry, at its height, is the Sun speaking. Language, when it mingles with spirit, does a tremendous service to the world: it empowers and changes lives; it awakens love, valor, wonder and reveals the Dance. The words of a poet-saint are unique. They become cherished friends to the heart, for they free—they constantly comfort and free.

People from many religious traditions believe that there are always living persons who are one with God. These rare souls disseminate light upon the earth and entrust the sublime to others. Hafiz is regarded as one who came to live in that Sacred Union, and sometimes he even spoke directly of that experience in his poetry. He offers secrets, *tangible keys*, to help those who are ready to integrate with God.

Someone once wrote to me, "How could anyone ever say they were God?" I replied, "If God exists, if a Real God exists—one of Infinite Power—then there is *Nothing* that God could not do. The physics, as it were, become simple: If God wanted, He could give Himself entirely to someone without ever diminishing His own state. And if you were the recipient of that divine gift—what would you then *Know?*"

Rumi, Kabir, Saadi, Shams, St. Francis and Ramakrishna are among the many known to have achieved perfection or "Union" because of their profound and intimate romance with the Beloved. They are sometimes called *Realized Souls* or *Perfect Masters*. In Hafiz's own words,

> *The voice of the river that has emptied into the Ocean*
> *now laughs and sings just like God.*

---

* This first appeared in one of my Hafiz books, *The Subject Tonight Is Love*, back in 1996, and was not used in later editions. I've got 14 raccoons I have been feeding lately, in this semi-tropical jungle patch of the universe where I often live. And I could've sworn the most wise of these beautiful creatures (their front-man) wanted me to put this in here . . . "Because we all love to hear *the Sun and the Moon speaking*," he said. "We know all about that, and wanted others *to know tooooooooo!*"

SELECT BIBLIOGRAPHY

Arberry, A. J. *Mystical Poems of Rumi, First Selection. Poems 1-200* Chicago: University of Chicago Press, 1968.

_____. *The Rubaiyat of Jalal al-Din Rumi (Translations from the Divan-i Shams-i Tabriz-i)* London: E. Walker, 1949.

Chittick, William C. *Me & Rumi: The Autobiography of Shams-i Tabrizi*. Louisville: Fons Vitae, 2004.

_____. *The Sufi Doctrine of Rumi*. Bloomington: World Wisdom, 2005.

_____. *The Sufi Path of Love: The Spiritual Teachings of Rumi*. Albany: State University of New York , 1983.

Kalchuri, Bhau. *Lord Meher: The Biography of the Avatar of the Age, Meher Baba*. North Myrtle Beach: Manifestation Inc., 1986.

Lewis, Franklin D. *Rumi Past and Present, East and West, The Life, Teaching and Poetry of Jalal al-Din Rumi*. Oxford, UK: Oneworld, 2000.

Meher Baba. *Discourses*. Walnut Creek: Sufism Reoriented, 1967; 7th rev. ed., North Myrtle Beach: Sheriar Foundation, 1987.

_____. *God Speaks, The Theme of Creation and its Purpose*. New York: Dodd Mead, 1955; rev. 2nd ed., Walnut Creek: Sufism Reoriented, 1973.

Nicholson, R. A. *Rumi: Poet and Mystic*. London: Allen & Unwin, 1950.

_____. *The Mystics of Islam*. London: Bell & Sons, 1914; reprint, Bloomington: World Wisdom, Inc., 2002.

_____. *Selected Poems from the Divan-e-Shams-e-Tabriz*. Cambridge: Cambridge University Press, 1898; reprint, Bethesda: Ibex, 2001.

_____. *The Mathnawi of Jalalu' ddin Rumi*, 8 vols. London: Luzac, 1925-1940.

Schimmel, Annemarie. *Rumi's World: The Life and Work of the Great Sufi Poet*. Boston: Shambala, 1992.

_____. *The Triumphal Sun, A Study of The Works of Jalaloddin Rumi*. Albany: State University of New York, 1993.

INDEX OF TITLES

I am a painter, a maker of the seen
and the hidden, 19
I died as mineral and became a
plant, 2
I have seen it happen when a
person dies, 14
I loaned existence its being, 102
I might have to slap my pencil a
couple of times, 51
I once heard that when the
Prophet Muhammad was
among us, 98
I relish good food, 6
I said to my Lord, "Never be shy,
dear . . .", 79
I saw my Beloved wandering
about the house, 34
I think I just want to be sad
today, 17
I think there should be some kind
of a checkpoint in books, 65
I travel with every caravan, 94
I was feeling a little down, 58
I would give my life for this, 101
If God just showed us His funny-
face more, 71
If someone tends us, we will be
like the orchard, 74
If the word father or mother is
spoken by a child, 48
If you are ever in need of a
kiss, 103
In a jungle this thick, there can be
brutal noises and acts, 80
It is a person's duty to get oneself
into a position, 24
It is for that minute when I might
steady you so you don't fall, 44
It is like an exquisite spider web,
this world, 10

It is not easy to find the grace that
makes an *extreme* lover of God
the way they are, 87
It decided to remain at a precise
distance from the earth, 38
It used to work this way: you
tidied up a bit, 59

Knowing of your great
accomplishments, 30

Left to its own ways, the snow
leopard will not move from its
kill, 20

Moments of happiness come to
lovers in their right mind, 36
Most everyone, all day long,
says and acts, "I am, I surely
am.", 85
My verse resembles a rare bread in
Egypt, 63

On this battlefield we have
entered, 100
Once Shams gave me a very
embarrassing hat to wear, 40
Once when I was asked these two
big questions, 93
Only late at night, when all the
kids are in bed, might God
come to earth, 77

Real spirituality doesn't turn one
into an *easy mark*, 12

Seeing how many miles you have
to go, 33
Some people punch a hole in your
being, 62

Someone might pet you more if
   you did not twitch, 68
Stars moving in other heavens,
   wanting to help those of
   faith, 18

Talking can be sweet. A field can
   bloom in your eyes, 45
That conch shell you crawled into
   on land, 32
The body is like Mary, and each of
   us has a Jesus inside, 3
The camel wakes after long
   journeying, 84
The physics would not be
   different, 31
The prairie's ablaze, 78
The rose is afraid of winter, 92
The scent of the rose garden, 9
There are a myriad different
   sounds in this world, 57
There have been thousands of
   things for you to pick from, 56
There is a golden bird living on
   the side of a cliff, 54
There is not a flood in all the
   worlds, 29
There is nothing wrong in looking
   forward to something, 50
These are like wedding vows, 46
They are like a lasting kiss, our
   sounds, 25
They come, those junctures,
   where it seems you must *turn
   right*, 35
They were expecting me, the
   plums, 11
Things are such, that someone
   lifting a cup, 27
This whole place is a man-eater, 88

Those precious words of hope that
   entered this world from our
   souls, 97
To my eyes, lovers touching are
   folded wings in a beautiful
   prayer, 81

Unless it is on drugs, or certifiably
   crazy, the fish, 64

Water says to thirst, "I am over
   here.", 52
We are like grain and life, the
   mill, 99
We just naturally turn toward her
   loveliness, 72
We started off pure gold, 82
What isn't booby trapped to
   explode if you don't handle it
   just right?, 69
When the old drunkard on his
   donkey cried out, 91
When the trouble comes, and it
   will, *O yeah*, 53
Who can I talk to but a yearning
   heart, 42
Why should I seek?, 5
With lightning coming from so
   many eyes, 28
Wonder and I took a vow, 70

You know about the holy, even if
   you won't admit it, 43
You might have noticed how
   animals may groom each
   other, 76